Lincoln Township Public Library
20...
St...

D0854980

# Michigan
## The Great Lakes State

Tika Downey

Lincoln Township Public Library
2099 W. John Beers Rd.
Stevensville, MI 49127
(269) 429-9575

**PowerKiDS** press.
New York

Published in 2010 by The Rosen Publishing Group, Inc.
29 East 21st Street, New York, NY 10010

Copyright © 2010 by The Rosen Publishing Group, Inc.

All rights reserved. No part of this book may be reproduced in any form without permission in writing from the publisher, except by a reviewer.

First Edition

Editor: Joanne Randolph
Book Layout: Kate Laczynski
Book Design: Greg Tucker
Photo Researcher: Jessica Gerweck

Photo Credits: Cover, p. 13 Altrendo Nature/Getty Images; p. 5 Richard Price/Getty Images; p. 7 © Heeb Christian/Age Fotostock; p. 9 © W. K. Kellogg Foundation; pp. 11, 17, 19, 22 (bird, flower) Shutterstock.com; p. 15 © Bill Pugliano/Getty Images; p. 22 (deer) © www.istockphoto.com/Bruce MacQueen; p. 22 (tree) www.istockphoto.com/Ling Xia; p. 22 (Henry Ford) Hulton Archive/Getty Images; p. 22 (Chris van Allsburg) Getty Images; p. 22 (Venus Williams) Getty Images Entertainment/Getty Images.

Library of Congress Cataloging-in-Publication Data

Downey, Tika.
  Michigan : the Great Lakes State / Tika Downey. — 1st ed.
     p. cm. — (Our amazing states)
  Includes index.
  ISBN 978-1-4358-9353-5 (library binding) — ISBN 978-1-4358-9802-8 (pbk.) —
ISBN 978-1-4358-9803-5 (6-pack)
  1. Michigan—Juvenile literature. I. Title.
  F566.3.D695 2010
  977.4—dc22
                                   2009026805

Manufactured in the United States of America

CPSIA Compliance Information: Batch #WW10PK: For Further Information contact Rosen Publishing, New York, New York at 1-800-237-9932

# Contents

BOOK ITA RM 10 6.2 25

# The Great Lakes State

Michigan is often called the Great Lakes State. Do you know why? It is the only state that touches four of the five Great Lakes! The Great Lakes are huge lakes on the border between the United States and Canada. Michigan has two **peninsulas**. People call the top one the Upper Peninsula, or the UP. The Lower Peninsula is shaped like a giant mitten! Can you find it on a map?

Michigan is famous for its wild places, cars, music, and for long, snowy winters. Have you heard of Motown? "Motown" is short for "Motor Town." It is a nickname for Detroit, Michigan, the nation's car capital. Motown Records, which is in Detroit, took its name from the city's nickname.

Michigan is a great place to do outdoor activities. These people are canoeing on Lake Superior, near Eagle Harbor Lighthouse.

People first came to Michigan about 11,500 years ago. The three main Native American tribes that have lived there since then are the Ottawas, the Potawatomis, and the Chippewas, also called the Ojibwas. French **explorers** began coming to Michigan around 1620. Jacques Marquette founded Michigan's first lasting settlement at Sault Ste. Marie in 1668. In 1701, the French founded Detroit.

The British took control of the area in 1763. After the United States became a free country in 1783, it took over the area that had been ruled by the British. In 1787, Michigan became part of the Northwest **Territory**. Michigan wrote its first **constitution** in 1835 and became the twenty-sixth state in 1837.

6

The French built Fort Michilimackinac at present-day Mackinaw City around 1715. For 66 years, it was the Midwest's fur-trading center.

Battle Creek, Michigan, is home to the Underground Railroad Monument. It is the nation's largest monument to the Underground Railroad. The Underground Railroad was a secret system that helped slaves escape to freedom in the mid-1800s.

People who led slaves to freedom on the Underground Railroad were called conductors. The groups traveled at night and hid in places called stations during the day. The people who hid them were called stationmasters. Battle Creek's two famous stationmasters, Erastus and Sarah Hussey, helped about 1,000 slaves escape. They appear on one side of the monument. The other side shows a famous conductor named Harriet Tubman.

The Underground Railroad Monument is 28 feet (8.5 m) long. Here, Harriet Tubman is shown leading a family of slaves to freedom.

# The Land of "Large Lake"

Michigan's name comes from the Chippewas. They called it *michigama*, or "large lake," because of the Great Lakes. Inside Michigan are many other bodies of water. The two largest lakes, Houghton Lake and Torch Lake, are in the Lower Peninsula. Lake Gojebic is the Upper Peninsula's largest lake. Between the two peninsulas run the **Straits** of Mackinac. Grand River is Michigan's longest river. The Detroit, St. Clair, and St. Marys rivers are important for boats carrying goods. The Tahquamenon River in the UP has famous waterfalls.

Michigan also has sand **dunes**, prairies, beaches, many islands, and low hills. The western UP has the Porcupine Mountains.

Here we can see the Porcupine Mountains and the Lake of the Clouds. Porcupine Mountain State Park is the largest park in Michigan.

# Michigan's Weather and Wild Side

Michigan's summers range from cool to warm. Winters are cold and snowy. Part of the UP gets about 21 feet (6 m) of snow yearly!

Many kinds of plants and animals like Michigan's weather. Forests with birch, aspen, oak, and pine trees cover half the state. There are frogs, turtles, and birds. There are porcupines, coyotes, bears, elks, moose, and even flying squirrels! Have you heard of the wolverine? This strange Michigan animal is not a wolf but a large type of **weasel**.

The official state animal is the white-tailed deer. It got its name because its tail is white underneath. The white part of the deer's tail can be seen when it runs. These deer can be found throughout the state.

An adult female white-tailed deer will give birth to one to three young each spring. The baby, or fawn, will lose its white spots by about five months old.

# Making Money in Michigan

Factories in Detroit, the nation's car capital, have made cars for over 100 years! Other Michigan factories make machines, rubber goods, and **green energy**.

Michigan has a lot of visitors every year, and there are many businesses in the state that take care of their needs. Visitors come for fishing, hiking, camping, and outdoor sports.

Other people work in Michigan's forests and farms. Maybe your family has chairs or tables made out of wood from the state's forests. Did you eat beans, blueberries, cherries, wheat, oats, corn, potatoes, apples, plums, grapes, or carrots today? Any of these might have come from Michigan!

This man is working in a Detroit car factory. There are not as many auto plants as there once were in Detroit, but it is still called Motor City.

# Let's Look at Lansing

Lansing has been Michigan's capital since 1847. At the capitol building, you can see Michigan's government at work. Lansing has many other things to see and do, too.

Do you like history? You can visit the Michigan Historical Center or learn about the history of **transportation** at the R. E. Olds Transportation **Museum**. You can also visit the Michigan Women's Historical Center & Hall of Fame.

If you like science, Lansing has plenty to see. At the Impression 5 Science Center, you can take a hands-on approach to learning about our world. A short trip to East Lansing will let you visit the Abrams **Planetarium**. No matter what your interests are, there is a lot to do in Lansing!

Michigan's capitol building, in Lansing, was completed in 1879 and has been in use ever since. The dome on top is made from a metal called cast iron.

# Lighthouses Along Michigan's Shores

Do you know what a lighthouse is? It is a tower with a very bright light that stands on a coast. In the past, lighthouses helped sailors find their way and told them land or rocks were near. Today, computers and other special tools have mostly taken the place of lighthouses. However, many people think that lighthouses are an important part of our nation's history and work to care for them.

Michigan has more than 120 lighthouses. No other state has so many. That is because Michigan's coast is more than 3,200 miles (5,100 km) long. That is longer than the distance across the entire United States! You can visit many of Michigan's lighthouses. Some have museums. Others will even let you spend the night there!

Grand Haven Lighthouse helps ships move around safely on Lake Michigan. The first tower was built in 1839 and the taller, second tower was built in 1905.

You can do all sorts of things in Michigan. There are beautiful lakes, beaches, forests, and wild animals. **Fort** Michilimackinac, the Henry Ford Museum and Greenfield Village, and the Gerald R. Ford Presidential Museum teach visitors about history.

Lighthouses along the coast offer beauty and lessons about the past. There are sports games, musical events, and the Motown Historical Museum, which tells the story of Motown Records. The famous Detroit Institute of Art has all sorts of art. Mackinac Island has the famous Grand Hotel, where visitors enjoy the lake and beaches and have old-fashioned fun. If you visited Michigan, what would you like to do?

# Glossary

**constitution** (kon-stih-TOO-shun)  The basic rules by which a country or a state is governed.

**dunes** (DOONZ)  Hills of sand piled up by the wind.

**explorers** (ek-SPLOR-erz)  People who travel and look for new land.

**fort** (FORT)  A strong building or place that can be guarded against an enemy.

**green energy** (GREEN EH-ner-jee)  The power to run cars and machines and make light and heat for homes and businesses that is made in a way that does not hurt the air, land, or water.

**museum** (myoo-ZEE-um)  A place where art or historical pieces are safely kept for people to see and to study.

**peninsulas** (peh-NIN-suh-luz)  Areas of land surrounded by water on three sides.

**planetarium** (pla-nih-TER-ee-um)  A theater with a domed screen used for looking at pictures of the night sky.

**straits** (STRAYTS)  Narrow waterways connecting two larger bodies of water.

**territory** (TER-uh-tor-ee)  Land that is controlled by a person or a group of people.

**transportation** (tranz-per-TAY-shun)  A way of traveling from one place to another.

**weasel** (WEE-zel)  A furry animal with a long body and short legs. Most weasels are small, but the wolverine is the size of a small bear.

# Michigan State Symbols

State Tree
White Pine

State Animal
White-Tailed Deer

State Flag

State Bird
Robin

State Flower
Apple Blossom

State Seal

## Famous People from Michigan

**Henry Ford**
(1863–1947)
Born in Dearborn, MI
Founder of the Ford
Motor Company

**Chris van Allsburg**
(1949– )
Born in Grand
Rapids, MI
Children's Book Author

**Serena Williams**
(1981– )
Born in Saginaw, MI
Tennis Champion

# Michigan State Map

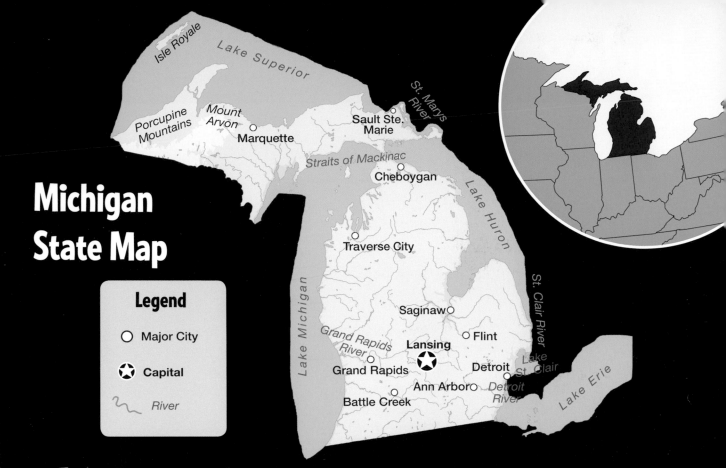

**Legend**

○ Major City

✪ Capital

〜 River

# Michigan State Facts

**Nicknames:** The Great Lakes State, the Wolverine State, and the Water-Winter Wonderland

**Population:** 10,072,000

**Area:** 58,527 square miles (151,584 sq km)

**Motto:** "Si quaeris peninsulam amoenam circumspice" (If you seek a pleasant peninsula, look about you)

**Song:** "Michigan, My Michigan," by Major James W. Long

# Index

# Web Sites

Due to the changing nature of Internet links, PowerKids Press has developed an online list of Web sites related to the subject of this book. This site is updated regularly. Please use this link to access the list:
www.powerkidslinks.com/amst/mi/